CAMBRIDGESHIRE BUSES

JOHN LAW

AMBERLEY

First published 2016

Amberley Publishing
The Hill, Stroud
Gloucestershire, GL5 4EP

www.amberley-books.com

Copyright © John Law, 2016

The right of John Law to be identified as
the Author of this work has been asserted in
accordance with the Copyrights, Designs and
Patents Act 1988.

ISBN 978 1 4456 5640 3 (print)
ISBN 978 1 4456 5641 0 (ebook)

British Library Cataloguing in Publication Data.
A catalogue record for this book is available from
the British Library.

Typesetting by Amberley Publishing.
Printed in the UK.

Introduction

The current county of Cambridgeshire was put together in 1974 and comprises three cities (Cambridge, Peterborough and Ely) and numerous smaller towns. It is mostly rural and flat fenland, although there are some smaller hills on the western and southern boundaries. Nevertheless, even the lesser-populated areas are well served by buses, partly because several of the towns (e.g. Wisbech, Ramsey, St Ives) have long lost their rail services. In addition, towns like March and St Neots are situated over a mile from the railway stations of the same name. Cambridge itself is famously a long distance from its station, allegedly to discourage the students from having easy access to the debauchery of London.

It was also around 1974 that I started visiting Cambridgeshire to take photographs of the local public transport. Since then I have returned many times, as I only live a few miles from the boundary and regularly worked in Cambridge and Ely.

The mid-1970s saw Cambridgeshire's buses dominated by Eastern Counties, a large National Bus Company (NBC) subsidiary based in Norwich and serving most of Norfolk, Suffolk and Cambridgeshire. Eastern Counties Omnibus Company (ECOC) was formed in 1931, a result of the amalgamation of several organisations. Two of these were Ortona Motor Company, based in Cambridge, and the Peterborough Electric Traction Company, running trams in that city. Cambridge never had electric trams, but had a small horse-drawn system, which could not stand up against competition from Ortona, and ceased trading as early as 1914.

The railways also had a large stake in ECOC, resulting in it becoming part of the Tilling Group, and have a standardised fleet of mainly Bristol/Eastern Coach Works buses, a policy that continued well into NBC days.

Prior to privatisation, ECOC was split up, with the western area forming a new company, Cambus. An insipid light-blue colour scheme, in NBC style, was initially adopted, but soon gave way to a bolder blue-based livery. Cambus itself was later split up, although it retained the same ownership. The Peterborough area operations became Viscount Bus Company, receiving yellow-and-white paintwork, although some buses carried Peterborough Bus Company names and a red colour scheme.

The very west of the county was very much the territory of United Counties, another former Tilling/NBC operator. This company had a depot in Huntingdon and a major presence in St Neots and Peterborough.

Both Cambus Holdings and United Counties became part of the Stagecoach empire in the 1990s. As part of the takeover, Stagecoach were required to dispose of their Huntingdon operations, which became Premier Buses for a short while, before settling on Huntingdon & District as a fleet name. By then the Yorkshire-based Blazefield Group was in charge, but it later sold out to local independent Cavalier. Stagecoach reacquired the business in 2008, trading as Stagecoach in the Fens and establishing themselves as the major bus operator throughout Cambridgeshire.

If this book just confined itself to the giant operators, it would be a rather boring one! Fortunately, there have been many independent bus companies to be found throughout the county. One of the larger ones was Premier Travel, who ran several routes from Cambridge, towards and over the boundaries with Suffolk, Hertfordshire and Essex, using a fleet of mainly AEC types. The company also participated in long-distance duties, many of which were retained after the stage-carriage routes were disposed of, under the name of Cambridge Coach Services.

Another bus company, now just a memory, was Burwell & District, with a smart brown-and-cream selection of buses running into Cambridge. The other major independent was Whippet Coaches, based originally at a depot in Hilton. Expansion took the fleet into a new depot off the A14 at Fenstanton, which was later passed on to Stagecoach after another site was acquired at nearby Swavesey. Whippet's territory has long been the area between Cambridge, St Ives, Huntingdon and St Neots. In 2014, by now trading as Go Whippet, the company was sold to Australian operator Tower Transit, although retained as a separate entity.

Other Cambridge independents have come and gone. Meridian Coaches briefly ran a tendered route, while Miller Brothers of Foxton started operating competitive services in the city after deregulation. These did not last long, with Cambus buying the bus services, while Miller Brothers renamed itself as Andrews Coaches, still trading today.

Cambridge is, of course, a great city for tourists, and open-top tours are a popular feature. A variety of companies have operated these, including Lothian Regional Transport, Young's, Ensign, and Guide Friday. The latter two also undertook brief forays into the stage-carriage market. City sightseeing tours are today operated using Stagecoach buses.

Peterborough has also been, over the years, a good centre to find independent buses. The best known of these is Delaine, based at the South Lincolnshire town of Bourne. A frequent service is operated, via Market Deeping, using one of the smartest fleet of buses in the country.

Another Lincolnshire independent to serve Peterborough was Kime's of Folkingham, with a service to Stamford and beyond. The service is now operated by Centrebus, providing a through route to Nottingham.

The service between Peterborough and the fenland town of Whittlesey was also in the hands of independent buses. While ECOC also ran buses along the route, a more frequent service was provided by Morley's, based in Whittlesey itself. This company sadly ceased operating in 2005. Alec Head, another local bus business, tried taking over the routes, but had no success. Canham's, with a yard in Whittlesey, also took some turns on the service into Peterborough, although this company no longer exists. The other firm to run between the two locations was Embling's of Guyhirn, latterly trading as Judd's Coaches; however, the license of this business was revoked in 2015.

Embling's ran into the small fenland towns of Wisbech and March, where other independents could be found. These have included Canham's (with a route between the two towns), Norfolk Green and Fowler's of Holbeach Drove, Lincolnshire. Fowler's no longer operate bus services, while Norfolk Green succumbed to the might of Stagecoach.

There have been many recent developments in the Cambridgeshire bus world. In the 1980s, two special services in conjunction with British Rail were introduced. One ran through to Kettering, a service now incorporated into the Stagecoach Gold route to Milton Keynes. The other went north-eastwards to Kings Lynn. This has now become the Excel X1 service, operated to a 30-minute interval to Norwich and the coast, in the hands of Firstbus.

One of the county's major trunk roads, the A14, has become busier than ever, with the expansion of Cambridge and heavy container traffic to the Essex and Suffolk ports. To counter the regular gridlock, the former railway line from Chesterton Junction, just north of Cambridge, to St Ives was converted into the Cambridge Guided Busway. Despite a lot of problems during construction, the busway was opened in 2011. The Busway also extends southwards to Trumpington Park & Ride site and Addenbrookes Hospital. Services along the busway are operated mainly by Stagecoach, with Whippet having a small share. Recent developments have seen busway services extended to Peterborough, via conventional roads.

Cambridge has also seen a rise in the use of park-and-ride services, in an effort to combat serious traffic problems in the city centre. These are operated by Stagecoach, usually by buses painted in liveries dedicated to each route.

Finally, mention must be made of a short-lived attempt by Peterborough City Council to run some local services in the city, using a small fleet of Optare Solos. These no longer operate.

In conclusion, I must thank my friend Richard Huggins for providing a few photographs taken at some more unusual Cambridgeshire locations. I am also grateful for those good persons at Bus Lists on the Web, who have saved me hours of trawling through my stack of fleet lists while researching for this book.

On 13 May 1974, we see Eastern Counties fleet number LS795 (4821 VF), a 1961-built Bristol MW6G, bodied by Eastern Coach Works, with thirty-nine coach seats (downgraded to dual-purpose duties). It is waiting in the small fenland town of Littleport to connect with a Bristol VR from Cambridge on route 109. The single-decker will soon depart for Kings Lynn on service 309.

Another Bristol MW6G coach with Eastern Counties. Number LS826 (APW 826B) was built in 1964, but carries a later style of ECW body, seating thirty-nine passengers. Painted in National white livery, it is seen in Cambridge, parked up on railway-owned land near the depot in Hills Road, Cambridge, c. 1975.

In the 1970s, Eastern Counties were still operating a few double-deckers with rear entrances. An example is LFS70 (70 DPW), a Bristol FS5G of 1963 vintage, with ECW sixty-seat bodywork and fitted with platform doors. It is photographed at Cambridge railway station in late 1977, about to depart for the city centre and Kings Hedges Road. A Bristol VR of United Counties is behind, about a mile into its long journey from Cambridge to Northampton.

Some of the Bristol FS5G buses of Eastern Counties were retained for driver training duties. Two are seen here, parked up near Cambridge railway station, in the late 1970s. FVF 422C and FVF 423C, both new in 1965, were originally fleet number LFS122 and LFS123 respectively.

The Bristol MW5G bus was a threatened species in the Eastern Counties fleet during the late 1970s. LM603 (AAH 103B) was delivered new in 1964, with forty-five-seat ECW bodywork. It is seen operating in the streets of the city of Peterborough in early 1978, passing along Bridge Street and heading for the bus station.

The late 1960s and early 1970s saw the Scottish Bus Group purchase several batches of Bristol VR double-deck buses. These did not find favour north of the border and soon made their way south, many in exchange for older Bristol FLF types. Eastern Counties took advantage to update their fleet. An example is fleet number VR333 (NAG 584G), an ex-Western Scottish VRTSL6G, with ECW seventy-five-seat bodywork. It is photographed in Cambridge's cramped Drummer Street bus station, parked up at a strange angle, *c.*1975. It could only be a Sunday – any other day and it would have caused chaos!

Another ex-Scottish Bristol VRTSL6G, new to Central Scottish Motor Traction, seen as Eastern Counties number VR319 (NGM 174G) in 1976. This seventy-seven-seat double-decker, photographed while not on service in Cambridge city centre, is seen close to the Market Place. It was being used as a publicity vehicle.

Here is an example of my favourite style of ECW bodywork. Sadly, not a large number of them were built. Eastern Counties RS649 (KVF 649E) is a Bristol RESL6G, built in 1967 and seating forty-six passengers. It is photographed in the small town of St Ives, heading for Somersham.

Another second-hand vehicle in the Eastern Counties fleet is seen in Drummer Street bus station, Cambridge, in 1980, about to depart for London. Fleet number LL837 (HRN 956G) is a 1969 Leyland Leopard/Plaxton Elite forty-nine-seat coach, new to Ribble Motor Services as number 956.

Another Plaxton-bodied Leyland Leopard coach is seen on the London service at Cambridge bus station in 1981. Fleet number LL839 (SPW 105R), again seating forty-nine passengers, was new to Eastern Counties in 1977. It is painted in an unusual version of the coach livery.

The half-cab Bristol FLF double-decker was popular in the Eastern Counties fleet, lasting into the early 1980s. This particular bus, number FLF434 (AVL 217C), was purchased from a fellow National Bus Company subsidiary, Lincolnshire Road Car. It is a standard FLF6G with ECW seventy-seat bodywork, photographed in mid-1980 at the parking area close to the River Nene and the old bus station in Peterborough. Some similar buses were also transferred from Eastern National.

A similar FLF6G, delivered new to Eastern Counties in 1966 as fleet number FLF443 (GVF 443D), is seen in the rather austere old bus station in Peterborough, on a quiet Sunday, *c.* 1977. This site was closed in 1982, being replaced by the present bus station incorporated into the Queensgate shopping centre.

The Bristol FLF6G buses of Eastern Counties in the Peterborough area ceased operating on the last day of 1982. Number FLF454 (JPW 454D) is seen on that day at Westwood terminus in the city's outskirts. I am grateful to Richard Huggins for taking this photograph.

Here is an early Eastern Counties Bristol LH6P with ECW forty-five-seat bodywork. New in 1968, number LH698 (RAH 689F) has the earlier body design, with a flat windscreen. It is seen on railway property near Hills Road depot in Cambridge, c. 1977.

Eastern Counties number RL735 (AAH 735J) is seen in Emmanuel Street near the bus station in Cambridge in around 1977. This 1970-built Bristol RELL6G, with ECW fifty-three-seat bus bodywork, is decorated in a special livery advertising the benefits of the company's parcel delivery service.

At the same spot, on a wet day in 1981, is another Eastern Counties single-decker in a special livery. Number RLE875 (YAH 875J) is a Bristol RELL6G with ECW dual-purpose body, seating fifty passengers. It is seen in a non-standard NBC red bus livery, lettered for the 'Cambridgeshire-Pick-Me-Up' rural service.

Eastern Counties number RLE744 (GCL 346N), a Bristol RELH6L/ECW, was a standard bus, but with forty-nine coach seats. It is photographed in National white livery on a winter's day in early 1982. The location is the old bus station in Peterborough, with the city's famous cathedral forming the backdrop.

The Cambridgeshire area of Eastern Counties was largely immune to the nationwide influx of minibuses of the 1980s (although Cambus received several batches). However, Ford Transit SVF 614N, given the fleet number X80, was purchased for use on specific services from Cambridge. It is seen outside Hills Road depot, in Cambridge, in January 1984. The vehicle was later transferred to Suffolk for rural routes around the small town of Eye.

1976 saw the delivery to Eastern Counties of a batch of nine Leyland Leopards with Alexander 'T' type forty-nine-seat, dual-purpose bodies. At the time, this was quite an unusual order, although other NBC subsidiaries also took some in. Fleet number LL754 (MCL 936P) is seen in standard NBC red-and-white dual-purpose livery at Cambridge station yard when almost new.

Sister vehicle LL753 (MCL 935P) is seen in Cambridge's Drummer Street bus station in early 1980, now painted in National white, although it is being used on bus duties. The spire of All Saints church is in the background.

This page features the standard buses of many NBC fleets in the early 1980s, particularly the former Tilling ones such as Eastern Counties. Number VR201 (WPW 201S), delivered in 1977, is Bristol VRTSL6G with ECW seventy-four-seat bodywork. It is caught on film in Cambridge bus station on a Sunday in early spring, 1980.

At the time, it seemed that the Leyland National was taking over every NBC fleet (with a couple of notable exceptions). Eastern Counties took over sixty of these integral-construction buses between 1973 and 1978. Number LN584 (TVF 619R) is one of these, built in 1977 with fifty-two seats. It is seen departing from the then brand-new Peterborough bus station on a local 'Speedline' service to Park Farm, in 1982.

The early 1990s saw several bus companies convert their Leyland Nationals to the East Lancs 'Greenway' specification, involving almost a complete rebuild. Generally a different registration was applied to disguise the actual age of the bus, but Eastern Counties, for some reason, kept the original registration on fleet number LN598 (WVF 598S). Delivered as a standard fifty-two-seat Leyland National in 1978, it was rebuilt in 1993. It is seen as a 'Greenway' bus in Peterborough bus station in the summer of 1994. By that date, Peterborough was very much Viscount Bus Company territory, so LN598 would soon return to its native Kings Lynn on route 794.

Much more suitable for the 794 service (now extended to Norwich) in spring 1996 is Eastern Counties number 26 (F613 XWY). New to Yorkshire Rider in 1988, this fifty-three-seat coach is a Leyland Tiger with Plaxton coachwork. It is photographed on its stand at Peterborough's Queensgate bus station.

Cambus was formed in 1984, from the western section of the Eastern Counties Omnibus Company. Initially a rather insipid light-blue colour scheme was applied, as demonstrated on fleet number 156 (GCL 347N), a Bristol RELH6L/ECW forty-nine-seat, dual-purpose vehicle. This was originally RLE747 in the Eastern Counties fleet. It is photographed in the bus parking area off Westgate in Peterborough, 1985.

In the same light-blue livery, Cambus number 611 (DNG 395K) is seen loading up at Cambridge railway station in 1985. Transferred to Cambus a year earlier, this 1972-built Bristol VRT/SL6G with ECW seventy-seat bodywork was new to Eastern Counties as VR395.

Cambus (ex-Eastern Counties) Leyland National, fifty-two-seater, bus number 203 (OAH 553M) is seen in St Andrews Street in the centre of Cambridge, around Christmas 1985. The ugly 1960s building to the right contrasts with the wonderful college building behind the bus.

Cambus number 632 (GHL 192L) is photographed at Cambridge railway station in the spring of 1985, still in NBC red livery. It had been previously new to West Riding as their fleet number 732. Built in 1973, it is a Bristol VRT/SL6G with seventy-four-seat ECW bodywork.

By early 1987 Cambus had begun to adopt a bolder colour scheme, which has been newly applied to a second-hand purchase at the recently constructed depot on the outskirts of Cambridge. Fleet number 806 (OBN 509R) is a 1977-built Leyland Fleetline, bodied by Northern Counties and new to Lancashire United, a most unusual vehicle to receive the two-tone blue livery.

Now given fleet number 70, GHL 191L is another ex-West Riding Bristol VRT/SL6G, with ECW bodywork. This one has been given a non-standard colour scheme, for its open-top tourist duties. However, it appears to be operating a normal city service, as it heads along St Andrews Street in Cambridge, en route to the city's Addenbrookes Hospital in the summer of 1990.

Cambus 501 (E501 LFL) is seen about to turn right from St Andrews Street and head for Cambridge bus station, in April 1989. This 1988-built Leyland Olympian has Optare bodywork, fitted with seventy coach seats. It was one of the first new double-deck buses purchased by Cambus.

Number 515 (F515 NJE) is another Leyland Olympian new to Cambus. Again, it is in St Andrews Street, Cambridge, in April 1989. This time it carries seventy-five-seat Northern Counties bodywork and was new only a month before the photo was taken.

New to Eastern Counties in 1978 as VR215, this Bristol VRT/SL3/6LXB with standard ECW bodywork has been given Cambus fleet number 723. Here BCL 215T is seen about to negotiate a tight turn in Peterborough's Queensgate bus station in early 1988.

Another ECW-bodied Bristol VRT/SL3/6LXB was photographed in High Street, Duxford village, on 26 October 1996. Cambus number 749 (DBV 28W) is a second-hand purchase, having been new to Ribble Motor Services in 1980. (Richard Huggins)

Cambus number 157 (L657 MFL) was only a couple of months old when photographed in December 1993. This Marshall-bodied Volvo B6, seating thirty-two passengers, is seen waiting for the barriers to lift at Ely station level crossing. Cars are allowed to bypass this bottleneck by utilising an underpass but, if the bus were to have done this, it would have emerged as an open-topper!

An identical vehicle to the one shown above, Cambus fleet number 169 (L669 MFL) is seen at Cambridge railway station in a dedicated City Rail Link livery in spring 1994. This bus was one of several Volvo B6 vehicles purchased to replace Optare City Pacers on the service to Cambridge city centre.

Cambus purchased several Optare City Pacers for local bus duties. Based on a Volkswagen LT55, these vehicles were designed to replace earlier Ford Transits and Freight Rover Sherpas in many fleet. This particular bus was new in 1987 to Taff Ely District Council, in South Wales. It is seen as Cambus S41 (E41 RDW), in the livery of Viscount Bus, in Peterborough bus station in late 1989. Viscount was the title of Cambus owned operations in Peterborough.

Viscount also had some larger vehicles from the Optare stable. Fleet number S2 (G802 OVA) is an Optare StarRider twenty-seven-seater, on a Mercedes 811D chassis, new in 1989. It is seen in the autumn of that year, when almost new, at Peterborough Queensgate bus station.

Viscount Bus number S11 (C521 DYM) is seen in Peterborough bus station in the summer of 1991. This twenty-one-seat Iveco 49.10 minibus, bodied by Robin Hood, was new to London Buses, where it carried fleet number RH21.

Here is a rather special vehicle in the Viscount fleet. Painted in the old Peterborough Electric Traction Company livery to celebrate ninety years since the founding of that organisation, it is seen in the sun at Peterborough depot on 20 July 1996. This standard Bristol VRT/SL3/6LXB with ECW bodywork, fleet number B50 (KVF 250V), was new to Eastern Counties as VR250. (Richard Huggins)

In later years, Viscount Bus also branded themselves as the Peterborough Bus Company, using a red-based colour scheme. In those colours is number B75 (PWY 45W). This Bristol VRT/ SL3/6LXB with ECW seventy-four-seat bodywork was new to West Yorkshire Road Car Company in 1981. It is seen in Peterborough bus station in the mid-1990s, bearing the name *Scarlet O'Hara*.

New to Viscount in 1993 is number S2 (K392 KUA), an Optare Metrorider twenty-nine-seat midibus. It was photographed here in the year of its manufacture on a local service in Peterborough Queensgate bus station. Albeit without fleetnames, it carries the Peterborough Bus Company red livery.

Much of the very western edges of Cambridgeshire were served by United Counties, a National Bus Company subsidiary once in the Tilling Group. A regular route was operated into Cambridge bus station, where we see fleet number 284 (TBD 284G) in 1974. Still in its pre-NBC dual-purpose livery, it is a 1969 Bristol RELH6G, seating forty-nine passengers.

At first glance, this is very much a standard bus from a National Bus Company fleet. However, United Counties number 750 (RRP 750G), 1969-built Bristol VRT/SL6G, has had its ECW bodywork rebuilt at the front, with its original flat windscreen being replaced by the later curved version. It is seen in United Counties territory in St Neots town centre, 1982.

United Counties had a depot in Huntingdon, clearly visible to train passengers on the East Coast Main Line. Parked outside on 13 May 1978 is number 622 (TBD 622N), one of several lightweight Bedford YRT/Willowbrook fifty-three-seat buses owned by the company. The Huntingdon depot eventually closed in 2009 and has since been demolished. (Richard Huggins)

In the few years between privatisation and takeover by Stagecoach, United Counties used an unusual livery for its 'Coachlinks' dual-purpose vehicles. Bearing this colour scheme is fleet number 601 (ARP 601X), a 1981-built Leyland Olympian with ECW bodywork, fitted with coach seating. It is seen at Cambridge railway station, near the end of its long journey from beyond Bedford, spring 1989.

In common with Stagecoach policy at the time, the local identities were retained, in conjunction with the corporate striped livery. In November 1989, 'Coachlinks' lettering has been applied to Stagecoach United Counties fleet number 645 (G645 EVV), seen in Peterborough bus station. The vehicle is a Leyland Olympian, delivered in September 1989. It carries Alexander R type bodywork, seating seventy-two passengers on comfortable coach seats.

Wearing Stagecoach stripes and United Counties identity, fleet number 738 (FDV 835V), a Bristol VRT/SL3/6LXB with ECW seventy-four-seat bodywork, is pictured here. It was new to Western National in 1980 and is seen in Peterborough bus station, heading for its Huntingdon home, in spring 1989.

Stagecoach later introduced a national numbering scheme and applied a corporate livery to its vehicles, which meant the end of the United Counties name. Carrying fleet number 16162, R162 HHK is in the latest paintwork as it passes through the Cambridgeshire village of Little Gransden on 23 February 2008. Transferred from the Stagecoach East London business, the bus is a 1998-built Volvo Olympian, bodied by Northern Counties.

Cambus and Viscount also became part of the Stagecoach empire in 1995. The company's logo can be seen above the driver's offside window on Cambus number 352 (N352 YFL), painted in Park & Ride livery. This Dennis Dart was delivered in 1996 with Alexander Dash forty-seat bodywork, and is seen here in Emmanuel Street, Cambridge, in autumn 1997.

Stagecoach Cambus number 301 (P601 JBU) in specially painted in a green livery for Cambridge
Park & Ride duties. This 1997-built Volvo B10BLE/Northern Counties forty-one-seat bus was
transferred from fellow Stagecoach subsidiary, Greater Manchester South. It is seen in Regent
Street, heading for Addenbrookes Hospital and Brabraham Park & Ride site, January 2001.

The Buttercross, in the centre of Whittlesey, is the main feature of the fenland town's Market
Place. It dates back to 1680, but the Stagecoach bus alongside was only built in 2001. Delivered
directly to the former Cambus operations, number 22306 (AE51 RYB) is a MAN 18.220 with
forty-two-seat Alexander bodywork. It was photographed on 5 September 2010, pausing for a
few minutes on its Peterborough–March journey.

The registration tells it all! Stagecoach Cambus number 82 (GAZ 4382) is a gas-powered Optare Metrorider, seating twenty-nine passengers. New in 1996, here it operates the free City Centre Shuttle in central Cambridge, autumn 1997.

In April 2003, pictured leaving Drummer Street bus station in Cambridge, Stagecoach number 32757 (L757 VNL) is a Dennis Dart with Plaxton forty-seat bodywork. This is a transfer from the Newcastle-upon-Tyne Stagecoach Busways operation.

Another transfer within the Stagecoach Group, Fleet number 34479 (PX53 DKF) is a 2004-built Dennis Dart SLF, with Plaxton Pointer bodywork. First delivered to Stagecoach (North West), it is seen here in Peterborough bus station, advertising the delights of the council's free childcare scheme, 9 February 2008.

Many of Stagecoach-owned double-deck buses in Cambridge are painted in dedicated park-and-ride liveries. In spring 2005, heading for the Trumpington site as it passes the bus station, 17008 (S808 BWC) is a low-floor Dennis Trident with Alexander bodywork. It was new to East London in 1999.

The X5 express service from Cambridge to Oxford, via Bedford and Milton Keynes, has proved very popular, running to a thirty-minute interval for most of the day. Heading for Oxford is fleet number 52486 (R186 DNH), a Volvo B10M-62 with fifty-one-seat Plaxton coachwork. It is seen passing through St Neots town centre on 15 July 2006. This vehicle was delivered in 1997 to the former United Counties, which was part of the Stagecoach business.

The vehicles used on the X5 are regularly updated. Number 53612 (KX58 NCE) and its sisters have now been superceded by newer coaches, delivered in late 2014. On 24 April 2013, it was still in front-line service as it passed through Eaton Socon, just across the Great Ouse from St Neots. En route to Oxford, it is a 2009-built Volvo B9R with Plaxton coach bodywork.

The City Sightseeing franchise in Cambridge is today operated by Stagecoach, using open-top buses such as number 16541 (ACZ 7489). This Northern Counties-bodied Volvo Olympian, built in 1996, was new to Cambus, with registration P541 EFL. It is seen outside Cambridge railway station on 16 August 2008, waiting for a few more tourists.

In a pink-and-maroon livery, designed to highlight the battle against cancer, is Stagecoach number 22060 (KV53 FAK). This 2003-built MAN 18.220 has Alexander forty-two-seat bodywork. It is seen in Drummer Street, central Cambridge, on 25 July 2012.

Stagecoach number 18337 (AE55 DJX) is seen operating a Cambridge 'Citi' local service, again passing along Drummer Street on 25 July 2012. This Dennis Trident/Alexander is in the current standard livery of the time.

The former United Counties operations of the Stagecoach Group are the owners of this bus, seen in Peterborough on 2 January 2015. Number 15401 (KX04 RCV), a Scania N94UD with East Lancs bodywork, seating seventy-five passengers, is seen in the special livery for local buses in Corby. It is well away from its normal duties!

Leaving Peterborough bus station on the X4 to Milton Keynes is Stagecoach 15744 (KX61 DLJ) on 24 August 2012. Painted in a route-dedicated livery, this bus is a Scania N23OUD with Alexander Dennis Enviro bodywork, capable of carrying seventy-two seated passengers.

With identical specification to the above double-decker, albeit with seventy-six seats, Stagecoach 15606 (KX59 BBN) carries lettering for the number 50 service between Kettering and Bedford. However, it is operating a local service in Cambridge, demonstrating the integration between the former Cambus and United Counties operations. Photographed at Drummer Street in the city, it is passing another Enviro on park-and-ride duties, 25 July 2012.

Stagecoach's Cambridge Park & Ride services are extremely popular, as car access into the city centre is very difficult. Each route has its own colour scheme. The Madingley Road–City Centre–Newmarket Road service vehicles are in red, as demonstrated by Stagecoach 19306 (AE07 KZH). This Alexander Dennis Trident 'decker, with dual-doorway Enviro bodywork, is seen arriving in the city centre on a sunny 25 July 2012.

Stagecoach Biobus-liveried 21230 (AE09 GZA) is seen on 25 July 2012, crossing the River Cam on Magdalene Street in central Cambridge. New in 2009, this bus is a Volvo B7RLE with Wright forty-one-seat bodywork.

Cambridgeshire boasts the world's longest guided busway, running between Trumpington Park & Ride site and Addenbrookes Hospital to Cambridge city centre and then along the course of a closed railway line to St Ives. On-street operation applies in the busy city centre, with bus priority schemes where possible. At Oakington and heading south towards Cambridge on the northern section of the guided busway, Stagecoach 15457 (AE09 GYD) is a Scania N23OUD with Alexander Dennis Enviro bodywork. Painted in the dedicated busway livery, the bus was photographed on 10 August 2011, only a few days after the official launch of the service.

Because of construction problems with the guided busway, the vehicles for the service were delivered long before the opening. Lettered 'I'll be on the busway soon, will you?' is Stagecoach 15461 (AE09 GYJ), identical to the vehicle above. It is seen in the small bus station at St Ives, on 12 September 2009.

When Stagecoach took over the United Counties business, the Office of Fair Trading was worried about the resulting lack of competition. Therefore, in June 1997, the Huntingdon area operations were disposed of to Julian Peddle, a well-known name in bus circles. The name Premier Buses was adopted and is seen applied to former Stagecoach 212 (K712 ASC), still wearing its old striped colours. This 1992-built Leyland Olympian, with Alexander bodywork, had been new to Stagecoach subsidiary Fife Scottish. It is seen approaching Drummer Street bus station in Cambridge, autumn 1997.

Blazefield Holdings took over Premier Buses in January 1998 and renamed the business as Huntingdon & District. A pleasant, if rather dated, blue-and-cream livery was adopted. Seen here on the Huntingdon inner ring road is fleet number 80 (DWW 930Y), an ex-West Yorkshire Road Car Company Leyland Olympian/ECW 'decker, bedecked in its new colour scheme in the summer of 1998.

During the years of Blazefield ownership, Huntingdon & District was effectively part of the Sovereign operation, based in Stevenage, Hertfordshire. Transferred from that neck of the woods and given fleet number 124, R124 HNK is a Volvo B10BLE with Wright forty-seven-seat bodywork. It is seen arriving in St Ives' town centre in late 2001.

Huntingdon & District number 4208 (H651 VVV) is pictured in the sun as it departs from Huntingdon bus station on 15 July 2006. New to Stagecoach (United Counties) in 1990, the bus is a Leyland Olympian with Alexander R type bodywork, originally fitted with coach seats, but now seen with less comfortable ones.

Another ex-West Yorkshire Road Car Leyland Olympian in the Huntingdon & District fleet, number 4211 (C479 YWY) is seen leaving Huntingdon bus station on 15 July 2006. This bus, with standard ECW bodywork, originally had coach seats, but is seen here with normal ones, perfectly suitable for the service being operated – the 666 to St Neots.

Huntingdon & District number 5320 (K916 FVC) is seen arriving in Market Place in St Neots, on 15 July 2006. This 1992-built Dennis Dart has Plaxton Pointer bodywork, seating forty passengers. It was new to Smith (trading as Your Bus) of Alcester, who used it on services to Birmingham.

Transferred to Huntingdon & District from Stagecoach United Counties was number 5316 (M430 BNV), a Volvo B6 with an Alexander Dash body, seating forty passengers on dual-purpose seats. It is seen in Huntingdon bus station on 15 July 2006.

Another vehicle transferred from Sovereign in Stevenage is seen heading for its new home as it departs from Drummer Street bus station in Cambridge on 11 August 2007. Huntingdon & District number 5310 (R123 HNK) is a 1998-built Volvo B10BLE, bodied by Wrights of Ballymena, seating forty-seven passengers.

This Huntingdon & District single-deck bus was new to another West Midlands independent, De Courcey of Coventry. Given fleet number 5325 (although this does not appear to be carried), R773 LHP is a Dennis Dart SLF, fitted with a Marshall Capital forty-seat body. It is seen at Huntingdon bus station, again on 15 July 2006.

In 2003, the Blazefield Group decided to dispose of its southern area assets, meaning that Huntingdon & District was sold to a nearby independent, Cavalier Coaches of Long Sutton, Lincolnshire. We will now look at a few of that company's buses, before seeing what happened later. Cavalier's AE51 VFU, a Dennis Dart SLF with Plaxton thirty-six-seat bodywork, is seen in March Market Place, in a council-sponsored livery, in February 2002.

UVG-bodied Mercedes O814D P164 XWO, in Cavalier hands, leaves Huntingdon bus station in autumn 2001. This thirty-one-seat vehicle was new to a South Wales operator, Williams of Crosskeys.

Cavalier's AE07 DZC is seen in the bus-and-coach park in Peterborough, on 18 June 2007. New only three months earlier, the bus is an Alexander Dennis Dart SLF, with forty-seat MCV bodywork. A Stagecoach Volvo Olympian/Northern Counties is parked alongside.

In March 2008 Cavalier/Huntingdon & District sold out to Stagecoach, renaming the whole operation as Stagecoach in the Fens. The Office of Fair Trading, after an investigation, agreed that the takeover was acceptable in September 2008 and Stagecoach corporate livery was soon applied to the fleet. However, on 12 September 2009, number 21165 (R125 HNK) was still in Huntingdon & District colours in St Ives bus station. New to Sovereign, this bus is a Volvo B10BLE/Wright forty-seven-seater.

Sister vehicle to the above, Stagecoach number 21160 (R120 HNK) now has its corporate colour scheme and looks very smart as it sits in the sun in the small fenland town of Ramsey. 4 June 2010.

The Nottinghamshire operator Barton Transport once ran stage-carriage routes into Peterborough, serviced by a small depot in nearby Stamford, Lincolnshire. About to head back to home territory at the old Peterborough bus station, *c.* 1974, is number 1249 (RVO 671L). New in 1973, it is a Leyland Leopard with Plaxton Elite Express fifty-three-seat coachwork, one of many purchased to update an ancient and ailing Barton fleet.

An identical coach to the one above, ex-Barton RVO 667L is seen in autumn 1991 at the new bus station at Peterborough. It is shown as number 367 in the Fairtax of Melton Mowbray fleet. At the time, Fairtax was a subsidiary of Midland Fox, which was a member of British Bus, later to become Arriva.

Arriva continued to operate into Peterborough for several years. Seen in the parking area in the city, fleet number 2149 (SJI 5569) is about to depart for Queensgate bus station and a tendered service to Maxey, January 2003. This Leyland National Greenway rebuild was new to Alder Valley as NPJ 471R in 1977 and rebuilt in 1994. After service with Arriva, it passed to A-Line of Warwickshire and was scrapped in 2007.

Although Delaine of Bourne still runs a Peterborough–Stamford service, many services between the two are now in the hands of Centrebus. The headquarters of that company are in Leicester, but it operates in many areas of the East Midlands and Hertfordshire. Centrebus number 670 (YH63 CXB), a VDL SB180 with a MCV thirty-nine-seat body, is seen in Peterborough bus station on 27 November 2013. It is about to depart for Oakham, in Rutland. Today, the route is extended beyond that and also now serves Melton Mowbray and Nottingham.

Despite Stagecoach having control of the former Eastern Counties operations around Peterborough, Firstbus (who took over in Norfolk) still run into the city on the X94. First Eastern Counties number 46 (N604 APU) is seen at Queensgate bus station in late 2001, just arrived from Kings Lynn and beyond. This fifty-three-seat Volvo B10M-62/Plaxton coach was new to Thamesway, the Essex operator, in 1995.

The X94 was later branded as the X1, the route number displayed on Firstbus number 20500 (AO02 RBX), photographed on 22 March 2008. This coach, a Volvo B12M with Plaxton fifty-three-seat coachwork, is seen in Wisbech bus station, wearing corporate Excel livery.

The X1 route from Peterborough to Norwich and the coast is now so popular that double-deckers are required. Firstbus fleet number 37574 (AU58 ECY), a Volvo B9TL with Wright bodywork, is fitted with seventy-four coach seats. It is seen arriving in Westgate, Peterborough, approaching the bus station on 25 August 2009.

The year 2013 saw new buses introduced on First's X1 Excel route, painted in a distinctive and smart new colour scheme. This is demonstrated by number 33808 (YX63 LJO), an Alexander Dennis E40D Enviro double-deck, sixty-seven-seater. It is seen loading up for Lowestoft, in Queensgate bus station, Peterborough, 27 November 2013.

Prior to the introduction of the X1 and X94 services, British Rail sponsored a connecting express service between Peterborough, Kings Lynn and Hunstanton. Painted in BR's blue colours is GEX 214Y, seen outside Peterborough railway station in spring 1984. Owned by Bird's of Hunstanton, the coach is a Duple Dominant-bodied Ford R1115, seating fifty-three passengers.

For a few years at the beginning of the twenty-first century, Peterborough City Council operated a few local services, using a small fleet of Optare Solos, such as 584 (MX05 OUF). This twenty-four-seater is seen departing Queensgate bus station on 15 April 2006. The council has now ceased operating these routes, but retains a small bus fleet for schools and social services duties.

The large independent bus company, Premier Travel Services Ltd, was founded in 1936. The business's bus operations reached parts of Essex, Suffolk and Hertfordshire, plus several routes radiating from Cambridge. The 1970s saw the AEC marque being favoured, with both new and second-hand vehicles being purchased. The latter included 319 NJO (fleet number 227), an ex-City of Oxford 1963-built AEC Bridgemaster, with sixty-five-seat Park Royal bodywork. It is seen in Cambridge bus station, *c.* 1975, on a service to nearby Sawston.

Another second-hand bus in the Premier Travel fleet, number 198 (VDV 796) was purchased from Devon General. New in 1957, this AEC Reliance has a Weymann forty-one-seat body. It is seen in Drummer Street bus station, Cambridge, in around 1975.

Premier Travel number 244 (OJE 550M) is seen in Drummer Street bus station, Cambridge, in 1976. Although fitted with forty-nine luxurious coach seats, this 1974-built AEC Reliance/ Alexander Y type is on a local service to Fulbourn, a village to the east of the city.

Number 254 in the Premier Travel fleet, registered JVE 373P, is captured on film in Cambridge bus station, spring 1981. This AEC Reliance, of 1975 vintage, has Plaxton Elite Express forty-nine-seat coachwork. It is loading up prior to an express journey to Birmingham, via Bedford and Northampton.

A scene at Drummer Street bus station in Cambridge in the late 1970s. As a Premier Travel Alexander Y type departs, number 256 (KVE 907P) in the same fleet takes on passengers prior to leaving on route 44 to Fulbourn. The coach is a 1976-built AEC Reliance with the latest Plaxton Supreme Express body, seating forty-nine passengers in comfort.

Premier Travel later adopted a smart silver livery, seen applied to three ex-London Transport DMS-type Leyland Fleetlines, not long before the demise of the company. The two buses on the left, KJD 24P and KUC 989P, are bodied by MCW, while KJD 116P, although seemingly identical, has a Park Royal body. All have been converted from dual-doorway layout and are seen at Premier Travel's depot in Cambridge. (Richard Huggins)

Premier Travel ran an express service from Cambridge to Oxford jointly with Percivals Coaches, with its own depots in both cities. At Cambridge bus station, in spring 1981, when both coaches were nearly new, numbers 81 and 79 (LWL 745W and LWL 743W) have just arrived. Although seemingly identical, these Leyland Leopard/Plaxton Supreme coaches have different seating arrangements. Number 81, having originally been ordered by a Staffordshire operator, Middleton's of Rugeley, carried fifty-one passengers, while number 79 found room for two more.

The village of Foxton, on the A10 south of Cambridge, was home to Miller Brothers Coaches. After deregulation, local bus service duties were undertaken. However, this photograph was taken *c.* 1978, when coaching was the main *raison d'etre* of the company. At the depot, on the left is PEB 127R, a Bedford YMT with Van Hool coachwork, while alongside is PER 57R, an AEC Reliance/Plaxton Supreme. Both coaches were purchased new in 1977.

After the introduction of deregulation, Miller Brothers introduced some bus services in Cambridge. A variety of buses was purchased for these routes, including XNK 209X, a Ford R1014 with Plaxton body. It was new to Ralph's of Longford, who had used it on airside duties at Heathrow – hence the offside door, locked out of use when photographed in Emmanuel Street, Cambridge, summer 1990.

Not all of Miller's buses were second-hand. F167 SMT was a Leyland Lynx fifty-one-seater, bought new in 1989. It is seen when almost new in spring 1989, passing along Emmanuel Street, Cambridge, having come from south of the city on a competitive service.

In 1992 the Miller Brothers business was sold to Cambus Holdings, with the buses used on Cambridge city routes retaining their separate identity. Photographed in summer 1994, F171 SMT (now given fleet number 312) is on park-and-ride duties at Emmanuel Street, in the city centre. Again this Leyland Lynx was new to Miller Brothers in 1989, though with only forty-nine seats.

Meridian Line, based in Bassingbourn, was a short-lived operator that gained a few Cambridgeshire County Council tendered services. MX07 OWU was obtained new for these routes and is seen at Drummer Street bus station on 11 August 2007. This Alexander Dennis Enviro 200 bus had a seating capacity of twenty-nine passengers.

Earlier in this book, we have seen that United Counties operated into the north-western part of Cambridgeshire. That company also ran several services around the small north Hertfordshire towns of Hitchin, Letchworth and Baldock. These included the sizeable village of Ashwell, again in Hertfordshire. One bus, however, was out stationed at Ashwell & Morden railway station, at least three miles from either village it purported to serve! It was also in Cambridgeshire. The southern section of United Counties later became Luton & District. Owned by that business, but with NBC-style 'Luton Bus' fleetnames, number 805 (PRP 805M) is seen at Ashwell station on 10 May 1986. It is a 1974-built Bristol VRT/SL6G with ECW bodywork. (Richard Huggins)

Like many similar cities, Cambridge had open-top buses offering tours of the local sights. The main operator of these was Guide Friday (see next page), but Lothian Regional Transport also entered the fray in response to Guide Friday's operations in LRT's home city of Edinburgh. Seen outside Cambridge railway station, in the summer of 1997, is number 21 (GSC 661X). Named *Fenland Star*, this Leyland Atlantean AN68C/1R was new in 1981 with a fully covered Alexander body seating seventy-six passengers.

Guide Friday's DWJ 564V is seen waiting for passengers at Cambridge railway station in April 1992. This ex-South Yorkshire Passenger Transport Executive Leyland Atlantean AN68A/1R with Roe bodywork has been converted to open-top format for its second life as a tourist vehicle.

Another Guide Friday owned open-topper on service in Cambridge. Daimler Fleetline RFN 965G was new to the East Kent Road Car Company in 1969, when it was delivered with a roofed Park Royal body. It is seen passing along Drummer Street in spring 1989.

Not all of Guide Friday's tour buses were open-topped. While it looks like it is a nice spring day in 1989, clearly some inclement weather was expected as MNU 191P passes through the centre of Cambridge. This 1976-built Daimler Fleetline, with a Northern Counties dual-doored body, was new to Nottingham City Transport as fleet number 191.

For a short period, Guide Friday introduced a stage-carriage service between Cambridge railway station and the Grafton shopping centre, via the city centre. An ex-Fife Scottish MCW Metrorider twenty-five-seater (F60 RFS) is seen on such a working at the railway station in September 2001.

A larger bus on Guide Friday's Cambridge city bus service is E114 KDX. Still in the livery of its previous operator, Ipswich Borough Transport, where it was new in 1988. This saloon is a fairly unusual Dennis Falcon, with forty-four seat East Lancs bodywork and a dual-doorway layout. Still carrying fleet number 114 and the name *Avocet* from its days in Suffolk, it is seen at Cambridge railway station in January 2003.

The Railway Station–City Centre–Grafton Centre route later passed to Cambridge Blue, part of the Ensignbus business. At the railway station on 8 July 2006 is number 108 (C808 BYY), a Leyland Olympian built in 1986, with ECW bodywork. It was new to London Buses as fleet number L8.

Cambridgeshire has long been the home of several coach companies, specialising in private hire, schools and contract work. One well-known operator was Young's Coaches, long based in Rampton, but today the company has its headquarters in Haddenham. At the old depot, *c.* 1977, is 7908 AC, a 1959-built Bedford SB1 with Duple Super Vega forty-one seat coachwork, new to Warwickshire operator Court of Chapel End. Alongside is former Barton Transport FVO 76D, a Bedford VAM5/Plaxton coach.

A vehicle new to Young's Coaches, YEB 105T, is seen at Rampton depot in 1983. New to the company in 1979, it is a Bedford YMT with Plaxton Supreme fifty-three seat coachwork. Alongside is the firm's open-topper, which features on the next page.

626 HFM was new to Crosville Motor Services in 1959 as a Bristol LD6B with ECW seventy-seat bodywork, convertible to open-top. Originally intended for tourist services in North Wales, it is seen here at Young's depot in Rampton, 14 August 1982. As can be determined from the lettering, it was used on Cambridge city tours. (Richard Huggins)

Young's Coaches had a pair of ex-Plymouth City Transport Leyland Nationals for schools and contract duties. SCO 423L and sister SCO 426L are seen at the depot on 14 August 1982. Both retain their dual-doorway layout.

Tellings-Golden Miller, having expanded from their Surrey operations, inherited some bus routes from Burton's of Haverhill, Suffolk. Seen at Cambridge railway station in January 2003 is X196 FOR. This Dennis Dart SLF, with Caetano forty-two-seat bus bodywork, was new to Geoff Amos of Daventry.

YM55 RRX is seen in Burton's livery, running through the village of Dullingham on 2 August 2006. New earlier that year, the vehicle is a Mercedes 814D, with standard Plaxton bodywork and seating twenty-nine passengers. Burton's went out of business in 2011.

Green's of Thorney ran a stage service on certain days of the week between the company's home village and the city of Peterborough. At the latter's old bus station, OEG 258M is seen waiting for customers, *c.* 1975. This Bedford YRQ, new to Green's in 1973, carries Duple Dominant forty-five-seat coachwork, fitted with two-piece folding doors, making it suitable for bus duties and thus attracting a government grant.

For a short period in the 1990s, Fen Travel tried operating competitive services in Peterborough. At Queensgate bus station in March 1995 is E84 OUH, an ex-National Welsh Freight Rover Sherpa minibus. A former City of Oxford double-decker, AUD 461R is a 1977-built Bristol VRT/SL3/6LXB with ECW seventy-four-seat bodywork.

Peterborough operator Gretton's Coaches was established as late as 1979, providing private hire and contract services to the company's customers. In the 1990s they owned a fleet of unusual Metro-Scania double-deckers, and one of these is seen on the busy A47 passing through Thorney Toll in July 1993. OCU 769R was new as number 769 in 1977 to Tyne and Wear Passenger Transport Executive, originally delivered with dual-doorway bodywork.

Shaw's Coaches, based in Maxey, a village to the north of Peterborough, runs a regular Spalding–Market Deeping service within the boundaries of Lincolnshire. The company's buses also make occasional forays into Peterborough, and this is where G23 UJR was photographed in December 2004. This Scania K93CRB, with fifty-seven-seat Plaxton Bustler bodywork, was new in 1990 to County Durham operator Armstrong's of Ebchester, near Consett.

One of Cambridgeshire's most well respected independent operators ceased trading in 1979, with the services passing to Eastern Counties. Back in 1975, when this photograph was taken, the fleet contained a fascinating mixture of vehicles. Inside the depot is 7552 MX, a 1962-built AEC Renown/Park Royal, new as an AEC demonstrator. Alongside is NLE 827, a former London Transport AEC Regent III with Weymann bodywork, new as fleet number RT3270 in 1953.

On the same occasion as above, YCY 803 was stabled at the depot. This AEC Regent V was new to South Wales Transport in 1961, when it carried fleet number 550. Bodywork, seating seventy-one passengers, is by Willowbrook, like many others ordered by SWT.

Burwell & District later favoured the Daimler Fleetline for its stage-carriage services. Seen arriving in Cambridge, *c.* 1976, is 9 DER. This Willowbrook-bodied example of the marque was purchased in 1963 and survived into preservation. Sadly, however, most of it was scrapped and all that survives today is the cab, an exhibit in Burwell Museum.

Another Willowbrook-bodied Daimler Fleetline in the Burwell & District fleet, bought new in 1965, was DEB 484C. This seventy-three-seater is seen in the cramped Drummer Street bus station in Cambridge, *c.* 1976.

Some of the Daimler Fleetlines in the Burwell & District fleet were purchased second-hand from Nottingham City Transport. These two were photographed at the depot in 1978. 63 NAU, on the left, carries Park Royal bodywork, while 87 RTO, alongside, has a Northern Counties seventy-seven-seat body.

Enterprise of Chatteris operated one or two services around the fenland area of Cambridgeshire. Seen on one such duty is D369 JUM, a Volkswagen LT55/Optare City Pacer twenty-five-seat minibus, new to London Transport as fleet number OV37 in 1987. This photograph was taken in December 1995, as the bus turns off North Brink in Wisbech.

Cambridgeshire independent Canham's Coaches once ran a stage-carriage service between March and Wisbech. On such a duty in 1973, we see VNO 866 crossing the railway line beside March station, about a mile from the town centre. The bus, a 1953-built Bristol KSW5G with ECW 'low-bridge' fifty-five-seat bodywork, was new to Eastern National.

Canham's Coaches, with its main depot at Whittlesey, also ran a regular service between that location and Peterborough, sharing the route with Morley's and Eastern Counties. On such duties, *c.* 1976, is USC 809, an ex-Eastern Scottish AEC Reliance/Alexander forty-one-seat coach, new in 1960. The location is the old bus station in Peterborough.

In March town centre, having arrived from Wisbech, *c.* 1975, we see 102 JTD in the hands
of Canham's Coaches. This fine vehicle is a 1959-built Dennis Loline with Northern Counties
sixty-nine-seat bodywork, new as number 7 in the Lancashire United fleet.

At the Whittlesey depot of Canham's Coaches is VER 560L, photographed in 1978. Built to
'grant-aid' specification, this Ford R192/Plaxton Elite Express forty-five-seat coach was
purchased new in 1972.

Also at Canham's Coaches depot in 1978 is EOO 589, a 1962-built Bristol FLF6G/ECW double-decker, new to Eastern National as number 1621. Alongside is Bedford SB3/Duple coach, a forty-one-seater (6 EBH), originally bought in 1958 by Soul's of Olney, Buckinghamshire.

Some vehicles in the Canham's Coaches fleet also carried Blue Bell Coaches lettering. Both names are seen applied to WEB 955L, photographed in Peterborough one night around 1978. New to Canham's in 1973, this Bedford YRQ has Willowbrook 002 bodywork, fitted with coach seating. Canham's Coaches ceased trading in 1983.

Another operator on the Peterborough–Whittlesey corridor was Morley's, based in the outskirts of Whittlesey. Several journeys were extended out into the fens to Coates and Turves. At Peterborough's old bus station, *c.* 1975, is UEB 782K, one of a pair of Bedford YRQ lightweights, with forty-seven-seat Willowbrook bodywork.

At Morley's depot, *c.* 1977, is NER 610M, a Bedford YRT with Duple Dominant coachwork, seating fifty-three passengers. It is fitted with folding doors to assist in stage-carriage work. Also in the depot are other examples of Duple-bodied coaches.

Morley's NER 610M is seen again, now in colour in 1986, when the coach was thirteen years old – a good age for a lightweight vehicle. A Ford Transit minibus is also seen in this view at the depot.

Another long-lived coach in the Morley's fleet. Seen in 1977, on the stage-carriage service at Peterborough, is BJE 474C, a 1965-built Bedford VAL14 with Duple Vega Major fifty-two-seat bodywork.

All the Morley's vehicles we have seen so far were bought new by the company. However, it was not unknown for second-hand buses to be purchased. An unusual example is NDP 38R, a Bristol VRT/LL3/6LXB with Northern Counties bodywork. New to Reading Buses in 1976 as one of its 'Jumbos', it originally carried fleet number 38. It is photographed in Queensgate bus station in March 1990, heading for Coates via Whittlesey.

Also new in 1976, this time to Scottish operator Western SMT, was NSJ 19R, when it was numbered 2602 in that fleet. It is seen enjoying a second life with Morley's at Peterborough bus station, February 1988. The bus is a Seddon Pennine 7, with classic Alexander Y type fifty-three-seat bodywork. Morley's ceased trading in 2005.

After the demise of Morley's, Alec Head of Lutton, Lincolnshire, took over the 701 service to Whittlesey, Coates and Turves. On such duties, leaving Peterborough bus station on 15 April 2006, is MCW Metrobus GYE 541W. This bus was new to London Buses in 1981 as number M541, when it was built to dual-doorway layout.

Another bus in the Alec Head fleet, G124 VDX, is seen in the parking area behind the Brewery Tap pub in Peterborough, in January 2006. It is a rare Dennis Falcon, built in 1989 for Ipswich Buses as fleet number 124. Typically angular East Lancs bodywork is carried, originally fitted with dual-doors. Alec Head soon gave up the 701 service, leaving the route to Stagecoach.

Lincolnshire operator Delaine of Bourne is one of the most respected independent bus company in the country. Services are operated into Peterborough, both from the Bourne area and from Stamford. Seen on arrival in Peterborough, *c.* 1975, is fleet number 65 (KTL 193F), a 1968-built Bedford SB5 with Duple Bella Vega forty-one-seat coachwork, adopted for stage-carriage duties.

Most Delaine vehicles, like the one above, are bought new. Occasionally, a bus was purchased from another source, particularly when that bus had not seen too much previous service. A good example is this former Maidstone Borough Transport Leyland Atlantean AN68/1R with Northern Counties bodywork. EKR 151L, new in 1972, was disposed of by the Kentish operator after that business decided to switch to single-deck operation. It is seen in Delaine livery, in Peterborough, *c.* 1977. Fleet number 80 is carried.

It is a crisp winter's day at Peterborough bus station on 9 February 2008, and Delaine number 128 (S5 OCT) is posed nicely in the sun. New to Delaine in 1998, the bus is a Volvo Olympian with East Lancs eighty-seat bodywork.

The low-floor bus has now arrived in the smart Delaine fleet. Number 135 (Y8 OCT) is a 2001-built Volvo B7TL, again bodied by East Lancs, this time with a capacity of seventy-six seated passengers. It is seen arriving at Queensgate bus station, Peterborough, on 25 August 2009.

Kime's, a Lincolnshire operator based at Folkingham, only started bus services around Peterborough after deregulation, with services out to Stamford and beyond, into the tiny county of Rutland. In 1997 the company became a co-operative owned by the employees. In summer 2000, Leyland Lynx YAZ 8827 is seen in Peterborough bus station, about to depart for Stamford. This vehicle was new to Luton & District as fleet number 400 and registered F400 PUR.

Kime's of Folkingham certainly liked their 'cherished' registrations! YAZ 4143 was originally M850 RCP, when it was new to Speedlink Air Services. This DAF SB220, with forty-nine-seat Northern Counties bus bodywork, is seen arriving at Peterborough bus station, December 2001.

Number S9 (AN09 BUS) in the Kime's fleet is seen in the later cream livery, with special lettering for route 9 to Oakham. Here it is at Peterborough on 2 May 2009, only a few days after delivery. This VDL SB200 low-floor bus has forty-four-seat Wright bodywork, to the latest design of the time.

Kime's also had a selection of double-deck buses over the years. Number D4 (GK04 NZU) was one of the last to be owned. This VDL DB250 with East Lancs bodywork is seen leaving the layover area in Peterborough prior to going on service, 11 October 2010. Less than a year later, the business was sold to Centrebus and that operator absorbed the services.

An operator based in Long Sutton, Lincolnshire, was Carnell's Coaches. A stage service into Wisbech was operated and it is that location which is pictured here, around 1977. Purchased new by Carnell's in 1972, this Bedford YRQ has Duple Viceroy Express forty-five seat coachwork and is registered TDO665K.

Wisbech now has its own small bus station. Just arriving here is G197 EOG, a Leyland Lynx forty-nine-seater, new to West Midlands Transport in 1990. The photograph was taken on 22 March 2008, three years before the company went into voluntary liquidation.

Another Lincolnshire operator that served rural Cambridgeshire was Fowler's Travel, based at Holbeach Drove. Awaiting departure for Wisbech in July 1993, at Parson Drove, is RNN 983N. New to Barton Transport as fleet number 1427, this is a Leyland Leopard with Plaxton Elite Express fifty-three-seat coachwork.

An unusual vehicle in the Fowler's fleet is seen at Wisbech bus station, 22 March 2008. New to Ulsterbus in 1991, as number 870, it is a Mercedes 709D. The twenty-five-seat bodywork was built in Northern Ireland, by Wright's of Ballymena. Fowler's Travel still trades, but no longer operates stage-carriage services.

The village of Leverington, just outside Wisbech, was once home to Coleman's Coaches. An interesting variety of vehicles was maintained. At the depot, *c.* 1978, is VUB 407H, a 1970-built Bedford VAM70 with Plaxton Elite coachwork. It was new to Woburn Garage of London WC4.

Barton was the source of several buses bought by Cambridgeshire operators. From the Nottinghamshire business came XAL 784, a 1957-built AEC Regent V with Northern Counties 'lowbridge' sixty-seven-seat body, fitted with platform doors. It is seen awaiting scholars in Wisbech, *c.* 1975.

Coleman's of Leverington had several double-deck buses for school contracts. Typical of these in the 1980s was AVX 973G, photographed at the depot, 24 September 1983. New to Eastern National, this Bristol FLF6G has standard ECW bodywork seating seventy passengers. (Richard Huggins)

Captured on the same occasion as above is ETD 946B. This Daimler Fleetline with Northern Counties seventy-four-seat bodywork started life with Lancashire United in 1964, when it carried fleet number 176. (Richard Huggins)

The large Cambridgeshire village of Somersham was once well served by its railway station. That situation changed in 1967 – thank you, Lord Beeching! Today public transport in the area is provided by several bus operators, including Dews Coaches, based in the village. Given an appropriate registration, BU52 ELY, this ADL Dart with ADL Pointer bodywork is seen in the city of Ely on 16 January 2010. It was earlier registered B1 JYM with its previous owner, Jim Stones of Leigh, Great Manchester.

Dews of Somersham ran a contract for Tesco supermarket using this ex-City of Oxford Volvo B10B-58 with Plaxton Verde bodywork. P630 FFC was one of several in the fleet when photographed in Ramsey on 4 June 2010.

Arrington is a village on the A1198 Royston to Huntingdon road, close to Wimpole Hall. In the middle of the village was the garage of George Jennings, who ran a few buses on contract duties. At the headquarters in May 1984 is UCK 527, a former Ribble Motor Services Leyland Leopard/Marshall bus. Seating fifty-three passengers when new, it was delivered as number 527 to Ribble in 1964.

Just off the aforementioned A1198 road is Bassingbourn, once the home of a famous RAF station. The depot of C. G. Myall was also based here and the company once ran a couple of stage-carriage services. Bought new for these was L452 UEB, a Dennis Dart with locally built Marshall bodywork, seating forty passengers. It is seen in Cambridge, on Chesterton Road, in summer 1994.

The famous East Anglian independent Norfolk Green's buses could also be found in the Cambridgeshire fens. At Wisbech in March 2005 is 235 (J535 GCD), a Dennis Dart of 1992 with Alexander Dash forty-seat bodywork. It was new as number 535 in the Stagecoach (South) fleet.

One of many Optare Solos in the Norfolk Green fleet, here is number 604 (Y58 HBT), a thirty-three-seat example. Named *Maggie Castleton* after a local character who lived in the fishing community of North End, Kings Lynn, the bus is seen in March Market Place, 17 April 2013.

The old railway station yard at Shepreth, between Cambridge and Royston, is the home of Kenzie's Coaches. No stage-carriage services are operated, but high-quality tours, private-hire duties and schools contracts are part of the company's portfolio. At the depot in 1983 is VAV 1X, a Kassbohrer Setra integral forty-nine-seat integral coach and the winner of the 1982 Coach of the Year Award.

A most unusual vehicle in the Kenzie's Coaches fleet was B948 ASU. Photographed at the depot on 26 May 2012, it is a Volvo B10M-56 with Van Hool bodywork. New in 1984 to Scottish operator Hutchison of Overtown as a fifty-one-seat bus, it was used by Kenzie's for school duties. (Richard Huggins)

First Choice Travel once operated some infrequent bus services around Peterborough. At the city's Queensgate bus station in summer 1996, we see E856 ENR, awaiting departure time for Maxey. This Volkswagen LT55/Optare City Pacer twenty-five-seat minibus was new to Leicester City Transport, who used it on 'Trippit' services in Loughborough.

Guyhirn is a village beside the River Nene, near Wisbech. It was home to Emblings Coaches, who ran several services in the area, including Wisbech–March. The company, sometimes trading as Judds Coaches, also had a share of the Peterborough–Whittlesey corridor services. At the depot in the late 1970s is CNR 16K, a Bedford YRQ/Willowbrook 002 bus, new to Gibson of Barlestone, Leicestershire. Alongside is Bedford SB5 coach RNK 128D, which started life with North Star Coaches of Stevenage.

New to Emblings in 1979 was Ford R1114 coach AEW 796T. Photographed at the depot not long after delivery, it has Plaxton Supreme Express fifty-three-seat coachwork. Keeping it company, to the right is a fine AEC Matador towing vehicle.

This fine vehicle, manufactured entirely by BMC in 2006, was originally new to a Scottish independent, McKindless of Wishaw. The forty-seat bus is seen waiting for passengers for Wisbech, in March Market Place, 17 April 2013.

The Peterborough–Whittlesey service was operated under the Judds name. Leaving Peterborough bus station on 27 November 2013 is L212 YCU. This Volvo B6-50, with Northern Counties thirty-nine-seat bodywork, was new to Kentish Bus in 1994.

Also bearing Judds fleetnames is E901 KYR, a Leyland Olympian with Northern Counties seventy-seven-seat bodywork. It had been new to London Buses' subsidiary Bexleybus in 1987. It is seen in March town centre, about to depart for Wisbech via Friday Bridge, on 17 April 2013. Emblings/Judds ceased trading in 2015.

One of the largest of the Cambridgeshire independent bus companies was Whippet Coaches. The business is still operating today, albeit since 2014 under the parentage of Transit Systems, an Australian-based concern. Founded in 1919, the company was based at Hilton, where this photo was taken *c*. 1974. On the left is KCH 106, an ex-Trent Motor Traction Leyland PD2/12, new in 1957 with a Metro-Cammell body. To the right is KEG 772L, a Volvo B58-56 coach, bodied by Plaxton and new to Whippet in 1973.

Whippet often used coaches on the stage services. An example is seen here in St Ives, around 1975. Bedford VAL70/Plaxton Elite AEG 564J is about to depart on Whippet's trunk route to Cambridge. This coach later saw service with Jenning's of Ashen, Suffolk.

Whippet Coaches had several former Leicester City Transport buses for school services. Arriving back at the new depot at Fenstanton in 1978 is 249 AJF. This Leyland PD3A/1 has Metro-Cammell seventy-four-seat bodywork. Whippet had moved to Fenstanton, just off the A14, in 1977. This site has since been sold to Stagecoach, while Whippet is now based in nearby Swavesey.

More suitable for stage services than the Bedford VAL we saw on page 91 is CAV 620V, by virtue of its 'grant-aid' doorway configuration. The 1979-built Volvo B58-56, with fifty-three-seat Duple Dominant coachwork, is seen loading in Emmanuel Street, Cambridge, in 1981. It will soon depart on a rural service to Papworth and Hilton.

Whippet Coaches also used double-deckers on their main stage-carriage services. About to depart from Drummer Street in Cambridge and head for St Ives is EAV 811V. Photographed in 1985 when the bus was six years old, this Leyland Atlantean AN68/2R has Northern Counties bodywork, capable of seating eighty-three passengers.

Another double-decker purchased new by Whippet Coaches was LEW 971P. This Leyland AN68/1R was delivered to the business in 1976. The bodywork, seating seventy-seven passengers, was built in Yorkshire by Charles H. Roe of Crossgates, Leeds. The bus is seen on its stand in Emmanuel Street in Cambridge, at some point in 1981.

A well-loaded G823 UMU leaves Drummer Street bus station, Cambridge, in the summer of 1990. New to Whippet Coaches in 1989, this Volvo B10M-50 Citybus has Northern Counties bodywork, fitted with eighty coach seats.

By 15 July 2006, when this photo was taken, the company had adopted the Go Whippet fleetname. This is seen applied to E911 DRD, as it departs from Huntingdon bus station. New to Reading Buses in 1988 (with the original fleet number 11), it is an Optare-bodied Leyland Olympian.

Go Whippet's L456 YAC is photographed in St Neots town centre on 15 July 2006. This Volvo B6-50, with Alexander Dash bodywork, was new to Stagecoach subsidiary Midland Red (South) in 1994.

Also purchased from the Stagecoach Group was K699 ERM, a Volvo B10M-55 with Alexander PS type forty-nine-seat bodywork. It had operated in the Cumbria area when new in 1992. The bus is about to enter Cambridge bus station on 25 April 2009.

Go Whippet now operate, along with Stagecoach, on the world's longest guided busway, mostly built on the trackbed of the Cambridge–St Ives railway line. Passing the site of the old station at Histon on 10 August 2011 is AE59 EHR. This forty-five-seat Volvo B7RLE with Plaxton Centro bodywork was bought new by Go Whippet for such duties in 2010.

Go Whippet's Plaxton Centros on the busway services have now been replaced by other buses. BG59 FYB is a Volvo B7RLE with Wright forty-three seats, new as a Volvo demonstrator. The guide wheels are clearly visible as the bus passes along Drummer Street in Cambridge, 25 July 2012.